The Connection Between the Bible and Secular Psychology

A Christian Therapist's View

Priscilla E. Pascual, M.S., LMFT

TABLE OF CONTENTS

DEDICATION

This is my special dedication to my parents, Melecio and Vicenta Fillon who left their children a legacy of faith in Jesus Christ. Their day-to-day witness of what it means to be a "light" in this world has been by example as their entire lives were lovingly devoted to those in need.

ACKNOWLEDGMENTS

Special thanks to my brother Pastor Samuel Fillon and my sister Rachel Sugimoto who have encouraged me to write and publish this work. Rachel is the one who first pointed me in the direction of becoming a marriage and family therapist and has cheered me on through the steps it has taken to come full circle. My brother, Samuel who recently retired from his pastorate after 50 years, supported this project as he has seen a need for a balance in the church with regard to secular psychology and Christianity.

Thanks to Claro, my husband and my sons, Jonathan and Reuben who journeyed with me through my schooling and my career. Thanks also to Isaiah and Elena, my grandchildren who will forever be my inspiration. I am so grateful to God for blessing me with them.

I want to thank God for allowing me to minister in this way. He has led me into places I never imagined myself going and into the lives and stories of people I will always remember.

INTRODUCTION

Growing up in a Pentecostal pastor's household, I had no feelings either way about secular psychology, as this was in the 1950s and to us therapy/psychology was basically unknown. I know my father did some pastoral counseling for marital concerns or other troublesome issues in parishioners' households.

When I decided to go into counseling as a career, I was in my 40s and serving in our small local church as a Sunday school teacher. I was absolutely grounded in my faith. I found that several teens I worked with had problems as some would stay after our class and let me know what was on their hearts. I would listen and would work with them as best I could, but felt limited in the help I was able to offer. I would pray, feel concerned, but that was about it. I mention prayer here because I pray and believe that prayer changes things. I also know that as humans we have our own will, and there are things in our lives which hinder prayer from working to its fullest capacity. We can pray but still run the traffic light and in cases like that, the laws of nature can and will prevail.

Upon sharing my career goal with a friend of mine who was a pastor, I had not given a thought to possible opposition to secular psychology/counseling and therefore I was taken aback by his response. He looked shocked, in total disbelief and scoffed at the idea. I soon found out that there were negative feelings about it in the Christian community. I began to be careful about letting people know what my career path was as I was not interested in debating the subject. However, as time passed and I got deeper into my work, I saw that it truly aligned with the ministry God has called me to do, which is to help those with broken hearts and those who have had their lives shattered.

There are churches with Christian Biblical counselors, and I would like to see more. People in the church are hurting and need good Scriptural guidance and comfort as society is ever-changing and can be a confusing place to be for themselves and their families.

If it were possible, more collaboration of helping professionals within and without the church would be profitable so that together we can be as effective as we can be to serve those in need. My mother referred to the church as an "emergency room at a hospital." All types of wounded are there as well as those with mental health issues. This needs to be acknowledged and plans must be put in place to help guide individuals into a place of healing.

There are more than enough hurting people to go around. Many people do not go to church and need services for counseling and mental health concerns. The cost of counseling from a private clinician can be exorbitant. Where can they go? Who can help them?

I have just completed almost 30 years as a psychotherapist, working mostly in community mental health. Throughout college, learning about different psychological theories and working with clients, I have been able to integrate my education with my Christian values without issue. I have discovered that Scripture supports principles I have used throughout.

At both major agencies where I worked, my managers knew I was a Christian and some were Christians as well. I also never once questioned my faith to follow a secular philosophy that could take the place of the Good News of Jesus Christ.

An employee who is a Christian should be a good example of Christ on the job daily and let their lives be the letter according to 2 Corinthians 3:3 (ESV). "And you show that you are a letter from Christ delivered by us, written not with ink but with the Spirit of the living God, not on tablets of stone but on tablets of human hearts." To me, this means that people may not pick up the Bible but when a Christian walks into another's life, the Word, Jesus walks in too.

As a Christian, I believe the Holy Spirit dwells within me, according to 1 Corinthians 3:16 (ESV). "Do you not know that you are God's temple and that God's Spirit dwells in you?" Wherever I go, the Holy Spirit goes as well. I do not leave Him at home when I leave for work. If I am going to work, He is automatically there with me.

"In the same way, let your light shine before others, so that they may see your good works and give glory to your Father who is in Heaven," Matthew 5:16 (ESV). Christians who are working in the secular arena of counseling can do this.

In this book, I would like to share some of the theories I have used or parts of them where applicable. This book is not an exhaustive review of any theory as that is not my purpose.

As in any career, like teaching, there are many theories and approaches to working with a student and delivering the material needing to be learned. In engineering, there are laws that govern how an airplane can fly, but different ways to get the desired result. A mental health clinician may use one theory or several and combine them where it is appropriate.

Biblical times are not the same as the time in which we live. Families were organized differently, and we are separated by culture, customs, time, and space. However, principles from Scripture can still be applied to today's individuals and families.

I will be using some of the relationships from both the Old and New Testaments as examples of relationships. My objective is not intended to force relationships in the Bible to fit with modern-day theorists on human behavior. I want to demonstrate how I worked in secular settings and was driven by principles of faith from Scripture and that other Christians can and have done the same thing without being conflicted.

Simply looking at the first couple in Scripture, Adam and Eve, we see dynamics at work which we see in couples today. Adam and Eve with the help of the serpent found a way to go around God's guidelines for them. In wanting more than what God had so bountifully provided, they were led into sin, shame and needing redemption from God. There was blame shifting between the couple with Adam going so far as to tell God it was basically His fault for giving Eve to him.

In the offspring of Adam and Eve, we see the struggle between Cain and Abel. Abel obeyed God's will for them, and Cain made the choice to go his own way. The competition between the two led to jealousy, anger and finally murder, all of which have been in humanity's lives since the garden.

CHAPTER ONE

THE GREAT COMMISSION

The Great Commission is Matthew 28:16-20 (ESV). Verse 19, "Go therefore and make disciples of all nations, baptizing them in the name of the Father and of the Son and of the Holy Spirit." These were the words of Christ to His disciples telling them to bring the "Good News" or the Gospel to all nations of the world. It also assures that when this was being done, He would be with them as they went.

The commandment of Christ to go into the world and bring the Gospel is a statement that should concern and be of primary importance to all Christian believers. The heart of the Gospel recorded in the book of John says that God sent Jesus to offer eternal life to all who would believe in Him. He also says in the book of Luke that He came to those who were sick and those who did not know there was hope beyond their present circumstance.

Entering the world of community mental health, I had the necessary degree to do the work, I met the training requirements for the state of California, and I took and passed the state examinations for my license. All of this was done as a Christian, and all in secular settings.

As a licensed therapist in California, I have laws and ethical guidelines that I must use and follow. We can do great damage to others if we do not practice within our scope of practice. One's experience and education dictate whom one may counsel.

I am not a Biblical counselor. I am not trained to be one. I do see my world through Christian lenses, however, as that is who I am, and use Scriptural principles every day.

Psalm 34:18 says that if our hearts are broken and our spirits are crushed, God is near us. During my career, I have only worked with those who are broken hearted, and their spirits have been crushed. As a therapist, I have heard about unspeakable abuse and neglect. Children have seen their parents killed right in front of them as a toddler did, watching his father die from the back seat of their car. These families go to programs that provide mental health in the community. They come to us.

I am a psychotherapist who is a Christian. My sister was a teacher in a public junior high school for decades. She is a Christian. One of my brothers was an aerospace engineer and he was a Christian. When Rachel, my sister applied for her first position, it was as an English teacher and music teacher as well. She brought the presence of Christ with her into this school and when the opportunity arose, she also sponsored the Christian club at that school for years. She let her light shine.

My brother, Reuben was the engineer. I know people used to challenge him for making "war machines" but he also brought Christ with him to work as when friends/colleagues expressed the need for prayer, Reuben was there to pray with and for them. Why did people allow Reuben to pray for them? Probably because he was already a good friend and colleague with whom they felt safe to share their burden.

(A therapist working with me had a small bottle of anointing oil in her car and worked in a program that allowed her to transport clients. One client saw the anointing oil in the car and asked the therapist to please come in and bless her home, anointing it with the oil. The therapist did. When the therapist came to see me for her weekly supervision session, she related the story to me. This was the client's request which came from her own belief system. The therapist did not bring this up, the client did, and made her request. The therapist and I processed what had happened, looking at options and concluded that in that circumstance she made the best choice in that moment. As I said, when a Christian goes to work, Christ goes with them. There was a trusting relationship in place. The client and therapist shared the same belief in anointing oil. It was part of the culture of both. Situations come up in relationships. We do the best we can with the information we have. Another therapist may have declined, but in this case my supervisee made a judgment call and followed what she felt was right.)

I knew from the start of my career that while I was to be a "light" to those around me, my job was to do psychotherapy as I was trained to do and to be the best supervisor that I could be to those who worked under my license. I was not seeing people in order to convert them to my faith or challenge their religious affiliation. I was there to assist with their mental health needs.

In fact, as a new therapist I was so good at compartmentalizing different parts of my life that when a supervisor of mine and I were speaking about a particularly challenging client, she surprised me with a question: "Do you ever pray for Bill?" Faith was a Christian and she knew I was too. My answer was "No." I had never thought of praying for my clients, and this one was difficult for me to treat and the less I had him on my mind, the better. Now, my supervisor who was a Doctor of Psychology was wondering if I included him in my prayers.

Faith knew that this client needed prayer. We did not go into a doctrinal discussion about this, but after feeling a gentle rebuke for not praying for him, it did open my heart to a more expansive role I had in my clients' lives: I needed to pray for them.

I have silently prayed during sessions many times and during supervision with my own team as well. I needed wisdom and guidance, peace, calm, understanding, and patience. Prayer is part of good counseling. I learned this is a secular setting.

CHAPTER TWO

INCREDIBLE YEARS CLIENT-CENTERED THERAPY TRAUMA-FOCUSED COGNITIVE BEHAVIORAL THERAPY

The theories from secular counseling which I have used throughout my career and most recently have been Client-Centered Therapy (Rogers, 2004) and Trauma-Focused Cognitive Behavioral Therapy (J. Cohen, A Mannarino, & E. Deblinger, Eds. 2017 2nd Edition). I am also certified in teaching parenting classes along with training in teaching social skills for children using *The Incredible Years* (Webster-Stratton, 2005), an evidenced-based treatment program created through the University of Washington.

In the parenting material, the basic principle we teach first is how to play and be with our children. This translates into engaging with our little ones, letting them know we love them and enjoy their company. Many parents when first entering the class want to know about disciplining interventions. They do not see the importance of starting at the beginning: building a loving, safe relationship with their child showing them that they are important and worth playing/being with each day.

As we are aware, if someone is loved, they are more likely to respond to what we say and know they are being instructed by someone who wants the absolute best for them. Without the solid "For God so LOVED the world…" of John 3:16 (ESV) the rest doesn't make sense. It is the same with Jesus and us, and us and our children. The foundation of loving our children and caring for them is vital to our relationships with them as they grow older.

Jesus talks about children in Matthew 19:14 (ESV) "but Jesus said, 'Let the little children come to me and do not hinder them, for to such belongs the kingdom of heaven.'" Jesus loves the children, and so should we.

I have used basic principles from various theories to do treatment and assessments as I conceptualized how a client came to be sitting in front of me for therapy. Secular theories can be used to inform clients on how they may have been impacted emotionally because of a divorce when they were toddlers or their own view of the world if they were separated from their family during critical periods of their development.

Through the years, I have seen how helpful these theoretical views can be in treating the wounded individual. As a Christian however, I know that along with therapy, ultimate healings come from God as He is The Great Physician, Jehovah Rapha.

(When my husband had open heart surgery years ago, they needed to replace the blocked arteries with healthy ones taken from his leg and one from his chest. His gifted surgeon was a leader in his field. After the surgery, I asked one of his assistants when the arteries would begin to mend. He said, "They have already started. When the ends are sutured together the cells immediately begin to connect to one another to heal." Amazing! While this surgeon did his part, God completed the process! True healing.)

Client-Centered theorist, Carl Rogers (Rogers, 2004) was a humanistic psychologist, and his contributions to the field of secular psychology are invaluable. He taught that people must be accepted for who they are and where they are at; that they should be in a relationship with someone who is genuine and who has empathy for them. He taught "Unconditional positive regard," which is found in Scripture, especially in the person of Jesus Christ. When I, as a Christian look at a theory, those principles which line up with Scripture are put to good use. I know that humanism begins and ends with the person without including God, and I know that as humans we are only complete when we have God in our lives in the person of Jesus Christ.

Thomas Gordon, Ph.D. (Gordon,1962) was a clinical psychologist who specialized in communication skills and conflict resolution. Again, genuine acceptance is an overriding principle here. As a counselor/therapist, one must convey during the first session that the client is welcomed and accepted. This is no small feat. Therapists greet clients with their whole being. We do our best to display open body language, genuine expressions of welcome, good, kind eye contact and words which convey warmth and safety.

A client's time must be honored by being prompt to session and ending session as scheduled. If a therapist comes rushing into session and is "running late" it sends the message that the client is being squeezed into this very important person's schedule. The client will take this cue from the therapist to "make it quick" and the client may go away with the thought that they are not valued, something they may feel from others every day. Therapists should offer a corrective experience, meaning that the client is offered something they have not felt before, which may be the first step in "correcting" the insecurities they are feeling.

We tell people we are accepting of them, but when someone appears different than us, automatic signals of non-acceptance may come up even before we are aware that they are present. Our non-verbal communication can be more deafening than the words we speak.

A client of mine years ago was telling me how she felt judged every time she had to go to court. Since a judge is present, this would be natural. Then she went on to list all others by whom she felt judged. I asked her, "Do you feel judged by me?" She answered, "Yes." With that out in the open, we began to talk about how this felt for her, why she felt judged by me and came to resolutions about how to move forward.

As a Christian, it is good to be in prayer when we are scheduled for any counseling sessions or meetings of any type. This is a good way to ground ourselves—meditating on Scripture and welcoming the Holy Spirit to be present with us.

As previously mentioned, at the most recent agency where I worked, our teams used Trauma-Focused Cognitive Behavioral Therapy (TF-CBT) (J. Cohen, A Mannarino, & E. Deblinger, Eds. 2017 2nd Edition). TF-CBT has several components, and I will speak to only a portion of them here: Psychoeducation, Relaxation, Cognitive Coping and Processing skills including the Cognitive Triangle. These components are used at the beginning of therapy and throughout to help the client regulate and remain stable as they go deeper into their work which includes processing the narrative of the trauma itself.

Psychoeducation is important in any type of therapy. It is the information shared with the client and caregiver to help them understand how traumatic experiences may have impacted them and how it manifests in the body and the emotions. In Trauma-

Focused Cognitive Behavioral Therapy, psychoeducation is the first key component in treatment.

It informs on why when you have been bitten by a dog for example, when you see a dog walking your way you may have a heightened negative response to the dog whether the animal is threatening or not. An individual may have had a punitive math teacher in junior high school, and if they see that math teacher again later, the same feelings the person had in the class years before come flooding back. Inadequacies the former teacher instilled in them remain. The client may not feel good enough or smart enough to deal with current issues even if the negative experience happened decades before.

I was working with someone and noticed that they struggled with getting their notes and paperwork in on time. They second-guessed themselves, reviewing something repeatedly to make sure it was right, even though their work was of high quality. I mentioned to them how I always reviewed everything and to please just submit the paperwork to me and if it was incorrect, I would let them know. I then asked them from where this drive toward perfection came. They said right away, "My former supervisor," who demanded flawless work. This supervisee was so impacted by that supervisor that their functioning was impaired going forward. It wasn't that I didn't want good work, but we can grow from our errors, and we all make mistakes. It is okay to be "good enough" as perfectionistic thinking can stop us in our tracks from finishing anything.

Looking at the life of Joseph, the son of Jacob (Genesis 37-50), it begins by stating that he was Jacob's favorite son and that his brothers were jealous of him. It is easy to see that while his life was guided by God, it was not an easy life and the family dynamics contributed very much to how his brothers reacted to him and he to them. Joseph sustained multiple traumas, all of which were life-threatening. He was going to be killed, then he was thrown in a pit, then sold as a slave, accused of rape, and put in prison where he was left to die. Forgotten.

If any of us had just one of those traumas, we would be a candidate for prayer and therapy. I have worked with families who have experienced community violence and have seen and experienced horrible things. We are living in a fallen world and are impacted daily by what we go through. Many of us, if any, do not have the relationship which Joseph had with God, and we are living in a different period of time.

There is an old saying, "Time heals all wounds." That is not true. I believe that Jesus can heal all wounds, but for some there will still be a scar. Our lives are not perfect, and God didn't promise us a problem-free life. In fact, He said, "I have said these things to you, that in me you may have peace. In the world you will have tribulation. But take heart; I have overcome the world." (John 16:33 ESV)

A therapist can help an individual realize that the anxiety, depression or other symptoms may be connected to something which happened in their past. They can let someone know how traumatic experiences do affect our emotions and our bodies. This can validate the individual so that the person is not alone to wonder if they are "crazy" or not. We are complex beings as the Scripture points out that we are "...fearfully and wonderfully made." (Psalm 139:14 ESV), and we are all different.

Psychoeducation can help normalize the symptoms and give people hope. Studies have birthed ways to deal with traumatic events helping clients live their lives without their painful history always cropping up and ruining their days. Psychoeducation continues throughout the therapeutic process to place things in context and give some understanding of what the client has experienced.

Psychoeducation can address the guilt and perhaps shame clients often feel when they are victimized. Many are young children who take responsibility for what perpetrators have done to them. Children are sometimes caught in the middle of domestic violence trying to defend a parent. If they are unable to do this, they may feel that they didn't try hard enough or may be afraid to say that they were immobilized by fear and could not help.

Unresolved trauma can follow a person throughout their life and may color whatever they see. An individual who has experienced trauma may withdraw, have impulse control problems with angry outbursts. They may be aggressive toward others or have trouble sleeping and eating. Victims may have intrusive, negative thoughts and flashbacks, which interfere with their daily functioning.

All traumas cannot be fixed, and while I believe trauma treatment models are helpful, they were not created to address the unbelievable and tragic experiences this world has to offer. I believe that many individuals bury the memories, if they can be buried, and just deal as best they can with what they have experienced. Some simply will not talk about their experiences as it may be part of their jobs like first responders, medical personnel, therapists, and of course, our military personnel, who have been amidst some of the worst experiences ever. People who work in these fields may talk to each other and process daily what they are feeling.

As we know, individuals react differently, and no one will have identical responses. We can all recall how someone has come through a challenging period and then continued with life as if nothing happened. Naturally, this is what we see on the outside. We often do not have a glimpse into their reality which may be well hidden.

Connecting with family and friends and having the support of an understanding community can make all the difference in the world. Having Christ to lean on and Scripture to meditate upon can give new meaning to each day. I cannot emphasize enough how difficult our world is to negotiate during times of war, uncertainty, civil unrest, and natural disasters. Humans can be fragile and if they need help, a good therapist can be seen and can introduce some new tools to use. Like open-heart surgery, only God can regenerate the severed pieces and truly heal the heart that has been injured, but a skilled surgeon, whom I feel God has provided for us, can initiate and assist in the process.

Relaxation is the second component of TF-CBT. When we have anxiety cropping up over a traumatic event from our past or simply taking a break in the middle of our day, it is important that we recognize when to take a breath and relax.

Sometimes we feel like to do God's work we must constantly be on the go. God knows we are frail and as my mom would always say, "I am just flesh with eyes," and we would laugh because we both knew what she meant. God understands our limitations, and He knows and cares that we are often feeling inadequate to face the tasks of the day.

Stopping ourselves mid-stream is difficult. We feel we must complete something, or we feel there is a loose end hanging. If we decide to do our deep cleaning of the house, garage, or the weeding of the garden, one individual will set aside a day and exhaust themself until it is done. Others will work on the same type of project for an hour and then set aside another hour the next day and so on until the job is completed. Most of the time, whatever works for someone is okay if it is working for the individual and not against them.

Sometimes when we are eating our lunch, we are moving so quickly through the process so that we can get to the afternoon chores or agenda. Mindfulness is a way to relax and is something that is very hard to practice but is needful. Mindfulness is used to bring us back to where we are in that moment and to peacefully reflect on what is happening with us and our surroundings. There is an admonition in Scripture Matthew 6:34 (ESV) which speaks to taking care of what is on our plate for that day: "Therefore do not be anxious about tomorrow, for tomorrow will be anxious for itself. Sufficient for the day is its own trouble."

We need to be mindful of Christ's presence with us. We should appreciate the beautiful sandwich at lunch, which is God's provision, thanking Him for it and for the enjoyment and nourishment it brings. This can bring a much-needed mini vacation amidst a stressful day.

The record of manna which was given to the Israelites is found in Exodus 16:1-36. This was supernatural food given by God to feed them while they were wandering in the desert. God gave express directions on how to gather this food which was to be "enough for that day." The overachievers, or perhaps greedy people, of course collected more than they needed and found out the next day that the manna was spoiled. We need to pay attention to what God says. Enough for one day was the command.

Learning to relax is important for everyone and especially for those who have experienced trauma. Individuals may have heightened responses to things during the day, as well as have unwanted thoughts from a stressful event creep in along with depression and anxiety. When we have ways to relax, such as deep breathing, mindfulness, or going for a walk, we can go to that tool kit and put those interventions into practice when we start feeling overwhelmed. There are many ways to use these concepts in counseling, Christian or otherwise.

Psychoeducation and relaxation are taught at the beginning and throughout therapy as needed. When a treatment session begins, relaxation can transition the client from what went on before session into a space that feels calm and serene. If the subject matter in session becomes too much, the therapist and client can agree beforehand to stop and do a few minutes of deep breathing, visualization or whatever the client chooses in those moments. Likewise, before session ends, grounding exercises can be done so that the client can be centered and balanced before going out the door.

I was seeing a 10-year-old girl whose parents were divorced. A conjoint session was requested to be held between the father and the child. The therapist of the father was present and before the father was asked to come into session, the other therapist and I were sitting with the child to prepare once again for the meeting. The child said, "Can we join hands in prayer?" The other therapist and I joined hands with the little girl, and she led in prayer before the session began. This was her way of getting emotionally balanced before the difficult session with her father began. In secular sessions, prayer can be used before session, during session and after session if a client requests it.

There is a "safe place" intervention I have used many times. In working with individuals, I have asked them to think of a place where they feel totally comfortable and at peace. To some it is their backyard garden, others it is the beach, and for some it is their mom's kitchen, with their mother cooking dinner. As they select a place, I ask them to remember the space, the colors, furniture, the aromas and the feelings they felt. For a Christian it may be their favorite chair, with their Bible on their lap, petting their dog on the head.

I recall my dad when he came home from work. He would change into his blue robe, sit at the end of the sofa where he was comfortable, and with his Bible on his lap he studied the Word. That memory is etched in my mind and heart, as my dad would sit there in that calm space that was totally his.

One of my safe places is at the beach. I love the majesty of the ocean, reminding me of the awesomeness of our Creator and the sound of the crashing surf, the smell of salty air and gentle breeze. I enjoy the colorful umbrellas during the summer and the sun shining through the clouds. I love looking at the dogs being walked and the small children riding their scooters as their parents try to keep up. I am alone in my visualization.

Jesus stated in Mark 6:31 (ESV), speaking to His disciples: "Come away by yourselves to a desolate place and rest awhile." He and His disciples were meeting the care and needs of the people, which at times became throngs. This had to be draining on all of them. Jesus knew how important it was to help his disciples be okay with taking a break as He also knew what was in store for these men as they followed Him. He was clear. Be alone. Get rest.

The book of 1 Kings 17-19 and 2 Kings 1-2 relates the account of Elijah who was an exceedingly colorful prophet who did spectacular miracles in Israel. He took his calling seriously and had challenging opposition from the reigning king and queen of Israel at the time, Ahab and Jezebel.

Elijah spoke to King Ahab and made a powerful statement as God directed him: "As the Lord, the God of Israel, lives, before whom I stand there will be neither dew nor rain these years, except at my word" (1 Kings 17:1 ESV). In the very next verse, God tells him to go to hide in a cave and that He would feed him and give him water. This is extraordinary. There was a natural brook of water in the cave and God sent ravens with food to feed him. All Elijah had to do was rest.

I can imagine how this might have been a challenge for Elijah. He was not one to sit; he was a person of action. He had nothing to do in that cave but eat, drink, and rest and let God provide for him. What a concept for individuals who have been wounded in life, or any one of us for that matter, that God can and will see us where we are and meet us there. First though, we need to stop and listen to him.

While Elijah did what God had said, God was also taking note of Elijah's need for special care. He was also preparing him for the next step, or task which was going to be enormous.

We don't know how long Elijah was in the cave, but it was a good while. How many of us would be wondering if this was really God's plan for us – to sit and do what seems to be nothing. Some people feel valued for what they can contribute or do for others. Some may feel useless if they have an entire day with "nothing to do." Our value is not tied to what we do, as Christ values us for who we are: His children, His creation. If this is not enough, perhaps this is something that individuals can look at in their lives. God expects us to work, to be industrious and to produce. But we are not valued because of these things. We need to simply withdraw from the chaos and renew our spirits. God knows what we need. Remember that we are more important to God than the tasks we do each day.

The day came however for Elijah to get up and go. In Chapter 19, Elijah was told by God to go and to challenge the worshippers of Baal and their prophets. When Elijah was there, it was a dramatic showdown and Elijah felt quite alone, thinking he was the only one left in the nation who loved God. His thinking was skewed by the opposition, and rightly so. Later God tells him that there were still 7000 who had not yielded to Baal, the false god of Ahab and Jezebel.

Our day-to-day life takes a toll on us and even Christians get tired. You don't have to be a prophet or apostle, but you are human, and fatigue physically, emotionally, mentally, and spiritually are all possibilities.

Years ago, when our children were young, we would do our shopping at the end of the week. At the market, there was a very lively checker who would cheerfully greet us and ask how we were. I was usually tired after shopping with two small boys, and so I would respond, "I am tired." She would then quote an uplifting Scripture, Philippines 4:13, telling me that Christ is our strength and basically rebuking me for being tired. I did not have the energy for this as I was being invalidated by this hyper-Christian woman who thought she was brightening up my week. Although I use Scripture daily to encourage myself, for prayer, for blessing, and for reminders about God's faithfulness, I did not need an exhortation from this individual at this time.

I began to dread going through this woman's line and while she obviously was trying to make me feel better, her Christian witness was just annoying. Therefore, we switched lines, hoping we would get a checker who was a "sinner."

When a young mother is tired, or a dad is tired, or anyone is tired, that may mean they have been working very hard that day or week or perhaps their whole lives. There is plenty going on each day to make us weary. We are not always on top of our game. When we end our day, we may be especially tired and wonder why. Then in reflection, we remember that the day started with a flat tire which made us late for our doctor's appointment and we were re-scheduled when we finally showed up. Remembering this will remind us why when we lay our head on our pillow, we are feeling overwhelmed and exhausted.

Imagine an individual with whom you are counseling who not only has their daily chores/jobs, children to raise, bills to pay but also intrusive, debilitating thoughts that hinder their day. That is a load to carry. There are people in the pews at church who can use your smiling presence to give them a lift rather than a condemning look when they are running late.

Cognitive coping and processing skills including the Cognitive Triangle are other components of TF-CBT. There are Scriptures that speak about our minds and the thoughts we have. Our minds are powerful. Proverbs 23:7 tells us that how we think dictates who we are.

Second Corinthians 10:5 (ESV) "We destroy arguments and every lofty opinion raised against the knowledge of God and take every thought captive to obey Christ." Sometimes we may feel condemned by thoughts we have. It is comforting to know that God knows our thoughts and although sometimes they are not the greatest thoughts, He understands and tells us that they can be controlled.

The thing about thoughts is that they are just that: thoughts. These thoughts can be challenged and replaced with thoughts that are helpful. Philippians 4:4 (ESV) speaks to this as Apostle Paul instructs us to "Rejoice in the Lord always, again I will say, rejoice." He also says not to worry about anything; instead pray about every situation. One might think, "Well that's a stretch." Yes, it is.

Negative thoughts are part of depression, anxiety, fear, and grief and can be addressed by examining our thoughts—evaluating them to establish what is true and helpful and what is not. God can help us to focus on Him through prayer and meditation, surrounding ourselves with knowledge of Him and thankfulness for His faithfulness daily.

The Apostle Paul also says to be purposeful in what we think about. Our minds often wander to the negative, the troublesome and soon we will take those thoughts, fuel our feelings with them and then produce negative behaviors. When we have thoughts that crop up, the first thing we can do is interrupt our normal process (if this is what we do) of thinking about it repeatedly. We need to stop that cycle. This is where we process our thoughts to see if they are true, helpful, false, or detrimental.

Therefore, when a client has been victimized and thoughts come to mind which can be debilitating, they can tell themselves to "Stop!" The individual may go back to the thought, but with the awareness that the thought does not have to control them. The client learns that they can combat the thought. Romans 12:2 (ESV) "Do not be conformed to this world, but be transformed by the renewal of your mind…"

Someone told me once that counseling does not work. You have heard about diet, exercise, and other things that require us to change if we want a desired result. Nothing works if we do not work. Counseling is not listening to a therapist once a week; it is what happens between sessions that will gradually transform an individual.

Transforming anything takes time. It is not accomplished quickly and will not be complete until we are with Christ. While we are in the flesh transforming is a day-to-day, moment-by-moment growth process until by God's grace, we can cast negative thoughts aside and replace them with praises to God for His faithfulness. In the past, I have used a worrisome thought to my advantage, as when I have the thought, I turn it into a cue that I can thank God in that moment for taking care of that situation. Praise takes its place.

The Cognitive Triangle speaks to how when we see something, we then have thoughts about it which then creates our feelings and eventually our actions. For example, I went into the waiting room to pick up a new client and when she saw me, she scowled. I was taken aback and immediately **thought,** "Is it my hair?" I don't know why I thought that ridiculous thought, but I did! I must have had a challenge that morning with my hair and wasn't satisfied with the result. Therefore, when I saw her response to me, in my mind I went right to my hair. Her look made me **feel** uncomfortable with my appearance and knocked me off center and as a result when I said "Hello" to her, I was **hesitant** in my approach.

As it turns out, she was angry because I was late for her appointment as the receptionist did not let me know she was there. It had nothing to do with my hair. It was because she thought she was overlooked by the receptionist. Her thought process may have been, "This receptionist is **ignoring me**, just like everyone else in my life. **I think** she does not like me. I am **angry** and will **complain** to the therapist when I see her."

A person who has been abused since exceedingly early in their life will see the world as a dangerous place to be. In coming to treatment, they can be taught about how thoughts can control their lives and how this does not need to be the case. They can learn about the Cognitive Triangle so that when they have troublesome thoughts, they can learn how to manage them.

As Christians, we are born again into a new life in Christ. We are to walk with a new eternal perspective, looking at things through a Biblical world view. It must be remembered that we are still a work in progress. We just have different goals, learning to follow Scriptural guidelines on how to walk each day. Things do not change overnight.

The Book of Acts records the story of the Early Church and of Peter and Paul who were two of the most influential Apostles and who could not have been more different from each other. They had to work together and transition from their old lives to a new way of thinking, acting and dealing with cultures which they previously were forbidden with whom to interact. They did not always agree as recorded also in the Book of Galatians, and their disagreements at some points made it necessary to go different ways.

Paul was a Roman Citizen, born into that status, and was a Pharisee who had a zeal for killing Christians. He was schooled by Gamaliel, one of the best, and had an authority and presence that he carried over into this new life after meeting Christ.

Peter fished for a living. He was not necessarily a learned person but was courageous and extremely devoted to Jesus when he was invited along with his brother Andrew to become a fisher of men. This is recorded specifically in Matthew 4:19.

The Scripture records the conflicts between the leadership of the early church with great clarity. Although their ministries took them in different directions, they were sold out to Jesus Christ, and He was always the center of their message. They were imperfect men doing their best to follow Jesus.

We are also imperfect, and it is not uncommon that disagreements arise in families and in church fellowships. It is important however to learn how to communicate with each other and to realize that in the process, we want Christ glorified in us although it may not always look so very pretty.

I am stating this here as it is important for our mental health and in our relationships that we let others know when we have been hurt or perhaps when we know we have hurt others. We may have misunderstood something said or perhaps misspoken and it is vital that no matter how unpleasant it is, we sometimes must bring up difficult topics that need to be processed.

CHAPTER THREE
ACTIVE LISTENING

Carl Rogers and Richard Farson (Rogers & Farson, 1957) speak to the issues of communicating which can maximize understanding of each other's needs and wants. Listening actively means that the hearer is focused on the other party: their words, body language, tone, etc. which convey what the speaker is trying to say.

The hearer's stance is open, non-judgmental, empathetic, and compassionate. Christian and secular counselors offer this to their clients. Trust between the two in this relationship is being built as the client starts to relax, lower defenses, and open their hearts to the hearer. The counselor is invested in understanding the person. If something is not clear to the counselor, they can stop the client and say, "What I am hearing is this, is that correct?" The client can then state that this is what they are conveying or clarify further for the counselor to fully understand.

As humans we are not always in a space to offer our partners, friends, congregants, children a safe place to express themselves. We do our best but often miss the mark. Jesus never misses the mark—He knows what we need even before we pray. These truths can be conveyed to the clients we serve.

A simple example of missing the mark can be a couple just getting home from work with the husband saying, "I am so exhausted." The wife, who may have had the same type of trying day may respond, "You had an exhausting day? You should be happy that you at least have adults to speak to! I have a classroom of third graders who were all on a sugar high!"

To the husband's statement, "I am so exhausted," the wife could have said, "Sounds like you are tapped out. Do you want to talk a bit about it?" The husband can then vent for a while as he was just validated by his wife that he worked hard that day. The husband can then say, "What about you? How was your class? I am sure that the kids were a handful as they normally are. I must hand it to you. You are so good with them. I do not think I could do what you do."

As I have taught many classes on how to speak to children and role-played active listening in sessions, I often hear, "No one talks like that. It feels funny to say that." And they are right. As a therapist, we can model better ways to communicate in session using words that the client is comfortable with. Matthew 6:9-13, Jesus taught the people to pray. The Lord's Prayer is prayed everywhere in the world by millions of people. This is not a comparison by any means, but our Lord lovingly guided people in the way to address and pray to Our Heavenly Father.

When we begin to change how we speak to others, it may seem like a foreign language because we are used to just saying a few words or grunting to acknowledge conversations that are being had. We make general statements to people, and no one knows who is being addressed. How many times have you heard at home, work or even church business meetings: "Some of you keep throwing your recyclables in the trash. Please do not do that anymore." This is to make sure that no one feels called out for doing something wrong or the speaker is too afraid to tell an individual to stop doing something.

There are ways to communicate something if you want to be clear. "Mary, thanks for keeping your work area clean. Let me show you where the recycling bin is."

Jesus knows each of us, even when we do not think anyone is aware of our existence. One day I had to go downtown to our headquarters, and as I entered the building I could look up and see a walkway across the entire room. Standing above me was a blonde lady dressed in a smart black dress, looking down at the floor below where I was standing. She said, looking straight at me, "Priscilla." Well, hello! I was caught off guard as I knew who this individual was but had no idea that she even had noticed we breathed the same air.

There is something powerful when someone calls you by your name. We are longing for relationships where we can really be known when someone is speaking to us and calling us by our name because they know and care. Jesus did this all the time, just as He did with Zacchaeus.

Jesus, the Master Communicator, the Master who loves us just as we are. Incomprehensible. Jesus would engage with anyone and asks the world to come to Him. He saw Zacchaeus up in a tree and stopped to speak with this man who just wanted to meet him. (Luke 19). Jesus also invited himself over to his house to share food. Jesus wanted to eat a meal with him! Zacchaeus was thrilled. He was not very popular with others, but Jesus saw past that and despite criticism, ate at his table. He knew how it felt to walk in Zacchaeus's shoes; knew how lonely he was without friends.

Jesus built a bridge to those who truly sought him, one of love and caring that they never experienced before. On the road to Damascus, Saul was blinded by a light and he fell off his horse. "And falling to the ground, he heard a voice saying to him, 'Saul,

Saul why are you persecuting me?' And he said, 'Who are you, Lord?' And he said, 'I am Jesus, whom you are persecuting' " (Acts 9:4-5 ESV). Although Saul did not know who Jesus was, Jesus knew exactly who Saul was and what he was doing.

Samuel Chapter 3 speaks about God calling Samuel when he was still a young boy. Scripture says that God didn't appear to many in those days and His Word was rare. Samuel did not know Who was speaking to him, calling his name, but God knew who Samuel was and delivered an incredible message to him. God sees us where we are. Zacchaeus was in a tree. Saul was on his horse riding to Damascus and Samuel was asleep in the temple. God knows our name.

Mary Magdalene was in the garden near the empty tomb of our Lord. John 20:11-18 talks about her encounter with the Living Christ, whom Mary thought was the gardener, until Jesus spoke her name, "Mary." There was no mistake when she heard her name. It was Jesus! We don't know why she didn't recognize Jesus at first, but it is beautiful that when her name was said, it made all the difference in the world.

When we speak, we need our clients, our family, our friends to know we are speaking to them. A good way to make sure that happens is by using their name.

I did group supervision for years and sometimes I had four groups with up to eight people in each group every week. At the beginning of every group, I would write down on my notes who was present. Of course, this was to keep track of attendance, but it also was helpful for me to have the names of the individuals in front of me so that I could look down for a refresher if I momentarily forgot their names.

Two best friends were seeing the same therapist for individual therapy. During session one of the friends noticed that the therapist was getting her confused with her best friend whom the therapist also saw. She was referring to Client B's story while doing therapy with Client A. When Client A told me this, I was appalled but the story is true. The therapist really did not know her clients in the way she should have. Jesus knows our story as He knows all things about us. He does not get us confused with someone else.

When people followed Jesus and were hungry, he fed them, met them at their place of need, and then taught them about who He was. He was teaching His disciples how to treat people, how to welcome them when they may have otherwise been turned away.

CHAPTER FOUR

ATTACHMENT

John Bowlby (Bowlby, 1997; Bowlby, 1988) is the leader in this field with Mary Ainsworth expanding the theory of attachment. The central principle again speaks to relationships between humans. This time it is the primary caregiver of a baby at birth, as the caregiver whomever that may be is the one who responds to the child's cries, need for food, warmth, and touch etc. As this infant grows, they learn that there is a dependable source in their world that will keep them safe and secure.

Years ago, at a conference which was focusing on early childhood, a speaker put a picture of a newborn on the screen. She asked, "What does this child need to live?" My mind went to survival as I thought of food and shelter. After giving us a moment to come up with our answers, she said: "The child needs someone to take care of them." Well, yes. I knew that. Everyone knows that. But do we know what that really means?

When I had Jonathan my firstborn, being a new mother, when we went out anywhere, I took the proverbial diaper bag. The bag held extra clothes, diapers, formula, bibs, wipes, a toy and whatever else it could hold. When my second child arrived, Reuben, when we would go out, I put a diaper in my purse and off we went. What changed? I realized that what Reuben and Jonathan needed to be cared for was their mother and father, loving them, carrying them, holding their hands and enjoying them. Things didn't really care for them—humans did.

A lot goes into the preparation of having a child. It can be complicated with rituals such as a gender reveal party where a unique way of the child's sex is revealed, or perhaps not assigning a "sex" until the child is old enough to do that themselves. There is the nursery, the live-in babysitter, the books to be read on "bonding" and a host of "how to" instructions on child-rearing.

While the unborn child is the supposed center of attention, it sometimes appears that some of the parents are adhering to societal pressures of the day, as the unborn child is just that: "unborn" and blissfully asleep in its mother's womb. He or she is being cared for in the God created warmth and security of their mother--nurtured by their mother. It would be wonderful if this continued after the child is born.

Caregivers can be dad, mom, grandparents, aunts, uncles, etc. These individuals can be the primary caregiver who is becoming the secure base or "go-to" person upon whom the child first looks to for care. I have worked with individuals who have been raised by nannies, and they have become the secure base for the little ones they have raised. The nannies in some cases are of a different socio-economic group or ethnicity, but the children attach nonetheless because that nanny has lovingly met their needs.

I had a supervisee who was seeing a client whose mother reminded my supervisee of the nanny who raised her. When it came time to separate from this client, the mother of this client brought the supervisee a small, inexpensive gift and the supervisee wanted to keep it. (We normally do not accept gifts from clients.) The supervisee had given the client a parting gift as well which is done especially with children "as a transitional object" or an object which will be a representation of the relationship and what it meant. As we worked cross-culturally, there were also cultural components to examine, but in the end as always, we asked "what does the gift mean?" In this case, as the supervisee and I spoke about the appropriateness of the gift we both knew that it was a small gesture to say "thank you" to the therapist.

I supervised a case—my supervisee was the therapist of a 14-year-old female who was the parent of an infant child. The client's name was Blessing. There was a meeting held determining the future of Blessing. Present were her social worker from children's services, their supervisor, the client's mother, and father who both appeared with their latest, current partners. The father's partner was pregnant, and the mother of Blessing had a small toddler sitting on her lap. The room was filled with adults, all there for the sake of this young teen mom.

Blessing was sitting next to me, and as I looked at her father and mother, I wondered to myself at what point was Blessing no longer a "blessing" to her family? I am not suggesting that these were not good parents, but I am suggesting that the warmth, security and nurturing of Blessing may have been interrupted amidst the complexities of her parents' lives. Both parents were on to their next partner and had new families. I sat there and tried to figure out where our client could fit into this mix. She did not fit. Just the logistics of the room told me and Blessing that there was no space for her. It was filled with concerned adults trying to figure out what to do with this 14-year-old, and as she observed it all, I can imagine how she must have felt.

There is an old saying, "The horse has left the barn." I have referenced this many times during my career. It simply means that the damage has been done. We cannot get the horse back. It does not mean that we cannot recover; it simply means that the path from point A to point B is going to be a challenging one.

The attachment in this family appeared to be there by the number of concerned individuals present. However, I was wondering when our client was left on her own to care for herself to bring her to where she was that day.

A good solid attachment is vital in an individual's life. As I have reflected on our Heavenly Father, and Jesus's message to Nicodemus in John 3:3 ESV, "Truly, truly I say to you, unless one is born again, he cannot see the kingdom of God," we are speaking about the need for someone who loves us, and who will care for us anew.

When we are born again, it is a new relationship, not a continuation of something old. It is altogether new. God is available to all of us, crushed in spirit, brokenhearted ready to be the secure attachment we all need and long for.

The theory of attachment teaches that a newborn's early years are of utmost importance. When a child is in the crib crying, the primary caregiver goes to the child and supplies them with food, a change of diaper, a warm hug, a gentle rock with an accompanying soft song, or whatever it takes to calm the baby. Babies learn that when they have a need, it will be fulfilled. In counseling of the Christian, it is the secure base with the Heavenly Father through Jesus Christ which the client needs to establish and build upon.

There is an old psychology film that shows a baby who is securely attached to their mother, crawling on the floor near her feet. The baby would go a little way and turn around to see if their mother was still there. Assured the mother or caregiver was there, the child grew more confident to go out a little further to explore. The child learned that as far as it went when they turned around, there was their secure base who would be available for any need that would arise. Trust is formed in these early years and the lack of trust in a caregiver can generalize itself to lack of trust in others.

Not all caregivers are a secure base for children. The child may see the caregiver, but when the child cries with a need, they are ignored. When they are hungry, they are not fed. When they need a diaper change, they are allowed to lie until the caregiver is ready to change them. What is this child learning from their caregiver? Perhaps, that they are not a priority, or that if they want to be safe that is something they will have to figure out for themselves, and that if they need to be soothed, they will have to find a substitute.

Matthew 7:9-11 ESV Jesus says, "Or which one of you, if his son asks him for bread, will give him a stone? Or if he asks for a fish, will give him a serpent? If you then, who are evil, know how to give good gifts to your children, how much more will your Father who is in heaven give good things to those who ask him!" What a wonderful promise for us. God knows what we need and will provide that very thing. He is forever our Secure Base.

There are good examples of parenting in Scripture. One of the most beautiful is the story of Jochebed recorded in Exodus chapter 2. She was the mother of Moses. Living in Egypt as a slave during his birth, this woman is a marvel to me. Although Jochebed was a slave, she lived in freedom because she was a child of God.

Jochebed became pregnant, and at the time all the male children born to Israelite women were to be killed immediately by the midwives. I wonder if Jochebed prayed for a baby girl. She had two other children already, Miriam and Aaron. The decree for male children to be killed was after Aaron was already born. As I mentioned previously, there are many plans which go into the birth of the child. There are many emotions positive and negative that accompany pregnancies. Jochebed was no exception.

She had a plan given to her by God. She made a little cradle or basket for Moses and waterproofed it. When he was born, she kept him until she could no longer hide him and muffle his cries. Can you imagine the heart of this mother who knew she would have to eventually place this little boy in this basket and float him down the Nile praying for someone to receive him into their loving arms? What faith she had in God.

When the day came, this is exactly what she did. Moses's sister, Miriam was sent by Jochebed to watch the little basket carry Moses down the Nile. The account in Scripture tells of how Pharoah's daughter was at the river with her maidens. She heard Moses's cries and saw him. She knew he was the son of one of the slaves-- one of the Israelite women. Miriam was watching the scene unfold and had the courage to go to Pharoah's daughter and offer her a wet nurse or lactating mother to feed Moses. Pharoah's daughter agreed and sent Moses back home with his sister, promising to also pay the nursing mother's wages! This was of course, Jochebed. God's provision.

Once again, Moses could feel the touch of his mother's skin, the fragrance of being in her arms and nurtured. Jochebed could feed her own child, soothe and caress him, all the while telling him what a miracle he was and how he was loved by God and his earthly family. What a wonderful God we serve. I always say that I am never surprised when God works, but I am utterly amazed at how His plan always comes together.

It is believed that Moses stayed with his mother and birth family until he was weaned, which would have been two to three years. In theory, these formative years are ones in which the child learns about his secure base.

From his birth home Moses then went to live in the palace with Pharoah's daughter. Everyone knew he was an Israelite, but it apparently didn't matter because God's will would be done despite all the odds against him. It's amazing that this happened as Moses was one of the boys which Pharoah made express orders to kill. Instead, decades later he was the great deliverer of all the Israelites from the cruel bondage of Egypt.

It appears that how one attaches in infancy can affect relationships throughout one's life. This of course is not the only contributor to how we negotiate relationships. However, it is another variable in our lives which shapes our views of the world: what we learn to expect from others and what not to expect. Our attachment can change as we develop, as we have a variety of experiences with other humans. For the Christian, as we allow God to work in us, we can learn to lean on Him as our Secure Base who can and will meet all our needs. We must trust in God, but that is easier said than done, especially for someone who has never experienced this before.

Other than Secure attachment, there are Anxious, Avoidant, and Anxious-Avoidant Attachments (Bowlby, 1997; Bowlby, 1988). The reader can research more on these styles. None are fixed, and as previously stated can change. Theories are ever-expanding as research continues and a theory can be proven to be wrong or can be adjusted as new scientific research is revealed. These styles can develop from inconsistent parenting, emotional or physical neglect or abuse. Basically, and this is very simplistic, in these cases, the child does not know what to expect from their caregiver and may wish to be independent of some relationships as they grow older if they cause too much distress.

For example, a child may give a gift to their parent for a special occasion, and the parent may appear disappointed with the present and complain about the item. They may overlook the gift without appropriately acknowledging the child's thoughtfulness in giving it to them. The child may learn from this that gift-giving to this parent results in emotional pain or hurt, something anyone would wish to avoid in the future. Therefore, they may cease buying gifts or experience much anxiety over purchasing something for this parent going forward.

A friend of mine was a product of a home in which there was a messy divorce and as a result there was the requisite division of time of the children between households. Holidays became cumbersome to this individual, and on one such day I asked where my friend was going to spend the day. Their answer was "at the park, alone." This was a "safe" place to be that they put in place to relieve themselves of the stress which came from spending the day with their family.

If someone has not felt loved, they may continue to feel unloved even if another individual pledges their love repeatedly. When children feel as if they are not a priority, they may continue with that view with others. Something as simple as a phone call not being returned immediately may tell them that they have been forgotten or will reinforce the lingering belief that they are not worth the call. There are those individuals who are fine in a relationship until the other individual becomes too needy (in their eyes or in reality) and the first individual may feel smothered by their partner. The first individual may then begin to distance themselves from the other as they are very uncomfortable being called upon for something that crosses their boundaries of protection.

CHAPTER FIVE

FAMILY SYSTEMS

Family systems looks at the client in the context of their familial relationships. When someone goes to therapy, there is usually the "Identified patient" or IP. This individual is the one that others feel has the issues and are singled out to get therapy. The thought maybe that if "Joe can just get himself together, the rest of us will be fine." Family systems takes a broader look and expands out from the IP to see the client in relationship with others in their world.

It is very important to get a good history from a client to see, as well as is possible, the environment where they were raised. There are the nature and nurture aspects that can be assessed as there are inherited traits and conditions which can contribute to the individual make-up of the client.

As an example, tendencies toward alcoholism can be traced to a parent, just as a person with musical talent usually comes from a family where people are musicians. An individual who has been adopted can easily have attachment issues depending upon the circumstances of their adoption. Pregnancies can be planned or unwanted and the birth of the child can be met with rejoicing as well as regret. All these variables can and will influence the child's formative years, his attachment to his caregivers, how they feel about themselves and naturally how they view their world.

I have often had conversations with other therapists about how challenging it is to treat children without also working with parents and other family members. The children leave their therapist and go back to their homes where they are at the mercy of the family dynamics in place. It is difficult for an adult to do this. With clients as young as 5 years old whom I have treated, it is almost impossible for them to take from what they have worked on in therapy and transmit that effectively into their family relationships where they basically have no power.

As we look at ourselves in context, we can see that we have been influenced by those who raised us, those from whom we learned, heroes in our worlds, our culture, race, ethnicity, and our sex. These are not the only variables. However, going back to Peter and Paul these men were also influenced by those who raised them, the environment, their skill set, giftings, privileges especially in the case of Paul. Peter and Paul were expected to work together after their calling to apostleship. However, they were humans with their own leanings and preferences and as God directed both without question, they were together in "spirit" but we may surmise not close personally.

Life is complex and living it is more difficult than it appears. When we become Christians, circumstances in our lives may be challenging, and the plus for the child of God is that we have Jesus as our Advocate who is always praying for us (John 17:20-23). We have His Holy Spirit (John 16:13) directing us through the thorns and thistles, distractions and temptations that come across all our paths.

Salvador Minuchin (Minuchin, 1974) speaks to the structure of the home as vital to a healthy family system. The family is made up of sub-systems such as the parental system, the siblings, and other members of the household if there are extended members present. When the structure of the family is upset then problems arise in the home. As is scriptural, the parents are the executive/parental system, directing the household, and the children are subject to that system.

Unfortunately, our world today appears to have a poor regard for the family as we have known it for years. In fact, families are not honored, fathers are absent, and mothers are gone as well. It is no wonder that when the family structure is gone, society is undermined, and children have been and are left to fend for themselves.

While it is preferable to have a mother and father in the home, working together to raise their children, we know that this is not always possible. Scripture points to the executive system of 2 Timothy 2:15. Timothy was raised in the faith by his grandmother Lois and his mother, Eunice. For some reason, Timothy's father is absent from the account.

This is a perfect example of how roles in families are played out, as when the father became absent, the grandmother stepped into a co-existing role with her daughter/daughter-in-law to parent Timothy. It is important in cases such as this that there is still someone in charge. In this home, Lois and Eunice had to agree upon where the ultimate power was held and that they both spoke the same thing to Timothy. The executive system agrees upon how things will be conveyed and what the expectations are in the home.

Ideally, the buck stops with whomever is the leader in the household, which is supposed to be the father. There is always room for discussion between the parents, but this is done out of the presence of the children so that when a decision is made, it will be presented by the parents as both agreeing and supporting the decision.

There are many views on leadership in the home, and who is the spiritual leader etc. Various churches and denominations teach different things, so the counselor will be consulting with their church elders to understand clearly how their fellowship interprets scripture.

When our family moved from Venice to Torrance around 1952, my mother voiced her opinion of not wanting to move because their home in Venice was paid for. My father on the other hand, had a vision of starting a church near Gardena and thus the decision to move to Torrance was made and completed. The blessings from this move went on for generations. My mother and father discussed these issues, and my mother followed my father's guidance. Mom was his helper as she was the one who negotiated things with the bank and took care of the business matters their entire marriage. They were an efficient unit.

When the sub-systems are pulled out of alignment, as when a parent dies or if there is a divorce, the system must correct itself to maintain its equilibrium or balance. If someone is missing, then someone else normally steps in to fill the gap. A simple example would be that if Janet usually takes out the trash and is gone, someone else in the home is designated to take it out. Similarly, if whomever normally does the cooking is absent, if the family wants to eat, someone else will cook or there will be a lot of takeout on the menu.

There are examples in Scripture of misalignment in the home. One of the most glaring examples is that of Rebekah and Isaac as recorded in Genesis 25 as Rebekah was aligned with Jacob her son, and Esau was aligned with his father. Each parent had a favorite. Instead of Rebekah and Isaac being the parental or executive system, their relationships with their children took precedence and a true family feud began.

Another example is that of the triangle of Abraham, Sarah, and Hagar. Genesis 16 and 21 records their story which was like a soap opera. God promised Abraham a son with Sarah, but God took too long. Sarah and Abraham had their own family meeting and decided to have Abraham try to have the child with Hagar, Sarah's maid. The result was a son, Ismael, but as is the case when we go about on our own to create God's plan for us, heartache ensued. God is a marvelous God whose compassion for us is beyond measure. In His time, God made something wonderful out of chaos, but it came with a price.

Families need order. A child in their early years has a schedule. They are bathed, fed, played with, and put to bed for sleeping at certain times every day. Babies need this as they begin to get used to their routine and they know what to expect. Please know that I am speaking from a "Western cultural perspective" since that is what I know. I cannot speak for other cultures as they are different, and what works in other parts of the world is great for them.

I went to a conference and the first thing the speaker said was, "What is the noise level in your house and what is your schedule like?" She was speaking about children with Attention Deficit Hyperactive Disorder. She basically said, "Look at your homes—how does your home contribute to a safe haven we all need from this busy world?"

We all need to be regulated. When we are agitated, we cannot focus or move forward efficiently to accomplish anything. We all have rules in our homes whether we know it or not.

We had childhood friends whom we played with everyday who had different rules in their homes than we did in ours. You may look at a home in chaos and say they have no rules. Yes, they do. The rule is "anything goes." If they want to clear the table after dinner, which was a rule in our home, they can or they can leave it as it is. Messy dishes from last night's dinner will still be on the table in the morning; condiments will all be out instead of refrigerated, etc. If we live a certain way, we will become used to it, and it will become our norm.

Children's temperaments/needs vary. Some children may appear to adjust better to an "anything goes home" than others. It is not unusual, however for an individual to say, "this is not how it should be done" and then make sure their area is cleared and clean before they will eat.

Someone told me that their parent would regularly beat them. At dinner, they were all expected to be at the table, bruises and all and no one said anything. This is another example of how we may live amidst chaos but are expected to respond as if we are not hurting and bruised or that we can eat despite disarray. Imagine trying to focus on homework, projects, or even fun activities, when living in such a fearful/unsettling environment. We are not in harmony with what is going on around us—we are incongruent.

CHAPTER SIX

TRAIN UP A CHILD

Proverbs 22:6 (ESV) "Train up a child in the way he should go, and when he is old, he will not depart from it."

In Deuteronomy 6 God outlines how we are to live. The chapter describes how a parent instructs their children about the things of God. It is assumed here that the parent does the training and teaching. Quite a formidable responsibility for parents. The Scripture assumes the parent and children are together. We know in today's world that we are not constantly with our children, but it appears that we are to maintain contact by some means throughout the days. Some families make it a point to have dinner together; others have family game nights; others integrate the children into doing chores or running errands. The Scripture infers that whatever you are doing, your example and your words show God's goodness to your children. The parent can explain to them about how God's faithfulness in the past will show them what He is doing today. In the Old Testament God asked that altars be built as memorials to events of God's goodness. These were to be reminders about deliverance, blessings, and promises.

When parents can stay close emotionally, spiritually, and physically, when possible, they can be the support and guidance in the world we live, especially when it is confusing for their children. In counseling, recommendations can be made to parents and families about ways to improve communication with their children and how they can incorporate God into the fabric of their lives.

I was at a church gathering once and a gentleman shared how his grown children would not attend church and how he needed prayer for them for this to change. Now, there are a host of reasons for children departing from church-going, even when parents have provided their very best God-led parenting they could. There is no judgment here. However, the gentleman went on to tell the small group present that he had been married three times and then began to describe how his last wife failed in their relationship. It is amazing to me how individuals must still wonder why their children have no interest in God when during their time with their children, they have gone through three wives and probably other relationships. Children learn from what you say but more from what you do.

A neighbor has a granddaughter who is about 2 years old. She was outside with her grandmother who was standing near her with her hands on her hips looking down the block. The granddaughter mimicked her grandmother with the same posture, hands on her hips also looking down the block. Our neighbor did not have to have a lesson on "How to Observe the Neighborhood" she simply went about her day with a very good student at her heels, though only 2 years old.

Another parent once said to me, "Mary's teacher called me today because Mary said a bad word in class." I said, "Where do you think she heard that?" The mother responded without hesitation, "I say it at home." No lesson here either on "How to Use Bad Words in School." Another child nearby learning the lesson of the day by simply observing what their parent did.

Years ago, I was at a family reunion on my mother's side of the family. My mom was Mexican, and the gathering was with hundreds of people, some of which I grew up with, others whom I did not know. My dad was a Filipino as my parents married out of their culture. My father was well-accepted in my mom's family and was known for his cooking. At this reunion, a woman came up to me and told me that when she was a young child, their family would come to visit our family and my dad would "cook up a storm." (Back in the day when people visited us, it was never a pre-set day and time, folks would just show up at our door.) She said that they were poor and when they came to our home, they knew that they would have a good meal. She said that they loved Dad's food, and we would all eat together, "after he prayed."

My father was a pastor as I mentioned earlier, and he and my mom were the best examples of how to truly worship God. They worshipped God as they fed this family who were hungry, and the family never left without Dad praying a blessing upon them. My father never preached at people when they visited; he welcomed them, fed them very well, with no judgment, and just a prayer. Our family was poor too—but our door was always open to those in need.

We learn from our family of origin how life is to be lived. It is important to note that children can be of the same family with the same training and still develop quite differently. Family members are individuals and will interpret and remember what they saw and heard from their perspective, view or lens they were looking through. What we learned and know is our version of how life should be lived. Everyone has a version.

Speaking earlier about the account in Deuteronomy on how to tell one's children about the goodness of God, is how my parents taught us. My parents would often say, "Look how the Lord has provided." I have used that with my children too, pointing to the faithfulness and provision of our good Lord Jesus Christ.

As we learned from our parents how to live a healthy life, there are also learned things that are unhealthy for us to continue doing. At some point, someone must make a right choice to stop the pattern of abuse, alcoholism, gossiping, etc., and by God's grace set a new pattern for the family to follow.

One of the questions asked during an assessment for suicide is if there has been a suicide in the family or of a close friend. If there has been, the client is at higher risk of committing suicide themselves. If the client has seen a friend opt out of life, there is that influence that this might be a choice for them too.

Murray Bowen (Brown, J & Christensen D., 1986) spoke to processes that continue from one generation to the next. Generational processes can be interrupted as a family member chooses to take another path rather than follow the steps of their predecessors.

Rebekah, Isaac's wife had a brother named Laban. As the story in Genesis 29 reveals, Rebekah deceived her husband Isaac as she and Jacob plotted to get the birthright which rightly belonged to Esau his older brother. Laban, later in life deceived Jacob when Jacob wanted to marry Rachel, Laban's daughter. Laban gave him Leah, her sister instead. Reviewing the way Rebekah and Laban operated, it may be that deceitfulness was part of their family's tradition as they saw nothing wrong with deceiving their own children as they felt the need.

Unfortunately, the deceitfulness of Rebekah and Laban was well thought out. Nothing was done in the spur of the moment, so one can possibly assume that they had done this before, and it was a part of their characters. It was also a legacy they left their children.

As the family narrative continues, Jacob's sons deceived him when they sold Joseph as a slave and then reported to their father that Joseph was dead. While in his youth, Joseph lacked wisdom it seems as he shared dreams from God with his family. The dreams showed him as the ruler he was to become over them and this, of course made matters worse. His brothers hated him already because he was favored by his father. Despite this, Scripture shows that Joseph followed God closely and in the end was the savior of his family and the entire nation of Egypt. This fulfilled the prophetic dreams. Someone must decide to do the right thing. When that happens, God is glorified amidst the most challenging circumstances.

Josiah the King of Judah was only 8 years old when he became king. His father and those kings before him were evil rulers but this young boy chose to follow in the steps of his ancestor King David. "He did what right in the eyes of the Lord and followed completely the ways of his father David, not turning aside to the right or to the left," 2 Kings 22:2 (ESV).

How remarkable! A child who had the heart of God, led the nation of Judah back to Him. In reading the account of the restoration process, we can see that Josiah *really* believed the Word of God. When Hilkiah the priest went to the temple he said, "I have found the Book of the Law in the temple of the Lord." It was brought to Josiah where Shahan, the secretary read it to the King. Josiah knew that moment that the people of Judah had not paid attention to the Law of God and had been disobedient. He was overcome with grief for himself and for his people and continued to purge the nation of Judah of all their idolatrous ways.

I am certain that Josiah received opposition, but he believed that following God was more important than those who wanted things to remain as they were. Josiah did not look to the opinion of others, as the Scripture says he followed "completely" the ways of King David.

Murray Bowen is credited with creating the genogram (McGoldrick & Gerson, 1985). A genogram is like a family tree and can be as simple or detailed as one prefers. I have used this as a means of gathering information on a client's family and can easily be a project for the client to do on their own or with their therapist. It is interesting when something is drawn out on paper; one can see the relationships and dynamics much easier. Physical ailments and other notable information can be inserted by the individual's name and through the generations on paper the client will begin to see trends and patterns.

I was working with a client who was physically abused by his father. As the client progressed in his genogram, he asked his mother about his father's upbringing as at this time his father was deceased. His mother stated that his dad ran away from home at age 14 because of being severely abused by his caregivers. This shed some light on why when his dad became angry, he took it out on my client.

Most family systems resist change. "We have always done it this way!" Some reasons for this are that the members of the system know what to expect, what role they play, how to respond or not respond to others in the system. When someone or something changes, it is unsettling and can easily divide a family.

I was told by an individual that at their family gatherings, someone always brought the chicken which was a staple at their special dinners. Well, the host one year created their own menu which did not include chicken. As the family members approached the beautiful buffet table someone asked, "Where is the chicken?" A battle royale ensued as the hostess said she wanted something different for this year's event. Many family members were incensed that she should make such a decision on her own, violating the standard expected menu others looked forward to having year after year. Chicken or the lack of it can cause an imbalance in a system.

My great-grandmother, Priscilliana Hernandez went to California from Texas when my mom was a teenager. She had an encounter with God and gave her heart to Christ. She went back home to Texas and brought the message of salvation, proclaiming, "I was blind but now I see." She changed the course of my mother's entire family, and all were converted from Catholicism to Christianity. Priscilliana had to be a very persuasive matriarch and her experience with Christ changed everything.

When my father came to the United States, he was 17 years old. He held various jobs, and at some point he became a migrant worker and lived in the camps with other Filipinos. They became his new family as he was relocated 10,000 miles away from his family of origin. My father lived the life of a bootlegger who carried a gun and smoked cigars. One day he was converted to Christianity, and he radically changed. He never looked back on his old life. His friends noticed the differences in my father and they didn't like the changes. He told them "When I used to box your ears you liked me. Now that I am living differently, you no longer want to be around me." What happened? Dad upset the balance in the relationships and his friends had to figure out how to respond.

Take the individual who wants to lose weight. Perhaps it is the husband who decides to "get in shape." His wife may need to lose a few pounds herself but is used to her way of eating. The husband may be following his new eating plan, and one day he walks into the house and there on the table is his favorite dessert. His wife may say, "You have been so 'good' on your diet, I thought you deserved a treat." As soon as the husband sees that he has a choice to make. He can refuse his favorite dessert and hurt his wife's feelings by not accepting her 'gift of love' or eat it and derail his eating program. A fight may ensue. Looking at this we must ask if this is really a gift of love? It may be the wife's way of bringing the family "back into balance" like it was before. Also, it would easily sabotage her husband's weight loss so that she doesn't have to acknowledge her own need for change and things can remain status quo.

These illustrations of families and change can be easily applied in counseling as we can help our clients evaluate their values/habits, trace where they have come from, and if they want to change their path. Clients can be validated in their struggles with others in their lives, they can problem-solve with the therapist on how to respond to opposition and find language to convey their needs.

In <u>Bowen Family Systems Theory in Christian Ministry, 2019</u> (Brown and Errington Eds, 2019) various individuals with leadership roles in their respective churches have authored essays evaluating Bowen's systems theory. Some applied it where appropriate in their own family system and in the system of their congregations. All authors of the essays have the Biblical perspective.

As Christians we submit to the Bible and acknowledge that we are all sinners saved by His grace. The Bowen theory on the other hand looks at the individual or IP and examines how the others in their world have responded to them, putting ownership of the relationship on the system rather than just the individual. Therefore, when things go awry the individuals in the system must look at themselves to see how they contributed to the dynamic. Some feel that this, however, would lead individuals to blame everyone else and release people of individual responsibility.

I believe that if members of a family or congregation are working toward the same goal, healthy individuals can examine themselves to see if there would be another way to handle a situation. This brings the Christian to the question of how their actions are contributing to the overall health of their family or to its demise. Or if they are being Christlike in their responses to one another.

Matthew 5 (ESV) records the sermon on the mount. In verse 44 it says, "But I say unto you, love your enemies and pray for those who persecute you..." This teaching is the opposite of what most of us do in these types of situations. This was also new to the people who heard these words from Jesus.

As mentioned in my introduction, we are separated from Scripture by space and time and live in cultures that have almost no resemblance to those in the Bible. There were arranged marriages, multiple wives and concubines and offspring from all which would lend themselves to various complex relationships. While we cannot apply Bowen's theory to say Jacob's family, we can certainly look at members of the system to see how they reacted or responded to each other.

Without getting into an argument between what the Old Testament and New Testament teach, let us just say that "people are people." While we are from different schools of thought on different subjects, we all are human and God's creation. We can say that we are more similar than not no matter what time in history we live or have lived.

CONCLUSION

Throughout my career, I have had the opportunity to pray for and speak with supervisees and colleagues about my faith as they have shared about a need for themselves or for their families. I didn't have to look for opportunities, as the opportunities came to me.

In the 1970s there was the Jesus Movement, and many had stickers on their cars that said "One Way" with a cross or another religious symbol. I had one on my car, and people would honk at me as I drove and point up to heaven letting me know that they were Christian too. I am not making fun of this type of witness but one night after getting home from work I asked my husband to take the sticker off my car. I simply wanted to drive home in peace. And so, he did.

There were and are business owners who would also have Christian symbols on their cards or advertisements as their witness. All that is fine and good. However, my thought is, "Do your job as it is expected, be kind to your customers, and don't cheat people" and your light will shine. Rather than announcing that you follow Christ at the onset, let folks know that you are a person of integrity, and they will see the difference in you. Then when you have an opportunity to share Christ your words will follow your deeds. There is a place for passing out Gospel tracks, sharing your faith at a bus stop or wherever God leads. But most of the time, our life is the witness.

"Go," means "you go." I go into the world. We are not of the world but look around you: we are in the world. Any career is filled with individuals who need Christ. How are we to reach them if we do not work with them and if we do not mingle with those who are lost.

The record of Philip and the Ethiopian Eunuch is recorded in Acts 8:26-40 (ESV). It says that Philip was directed by the angel of the Lord to go "down from Jerusalem to Gaza." Philip did as he was directed and met this man who was seated in his chariot reading from the prophet Isaiah. As Philip sees this, he asks if he understands the Scripture. Verse 31 says, "How can I unless someone guides me?"

This was a golden opportunity as Philip was able to share Christ with this hungry soul, and the Ethiopian was fed the Living Word. From the looks of this individual, he did not seem to lack anything. He was wealthy and in a chariot on his way back from worshipping in Jerusalem. All the boxes were checked. Although this man was not someone Philip knew from his own segment of society, he was still sent to share the Gospel with him into the world of this Ethiopian, which was very different than Philip's.

At the beginning of my journey working in mental health, I had no idea that I would be enriched and blessed beyond measure. I have truly reaped much more than I have sown, all by God's grace.

As Christians, we do not have to reject working in a secular community of psychology because it is not necessarily Christ-centered. We however are centered firmly in Christ and that is what matters. We can also be confident in the fact that the Bible can work in harmony with concepts from secular psychology.

However, if you believe that this is not your calling, then do not do it. My dad was incredibly wise. When he would share a spiritual insight with us, he knew that this was not something for everyone. He would say, "Do not make it a doctrine." Which meant: "This is coming from me, and it has merit. It is not, however the Holy Scripture."

These are my thoughts following my experience after almost 30 years working in secular psychology. I did not forge this path alone, as I know that this was God's will for me. There are many ways to serve God with our lives and God has the plan fit especially for you too.

Where does our light shine? It shines brightest in dark places. My mom would often say, "the Lily of the Valley shines brightest in the valley." We are in the valley every day that we live in our troubled world. Therefore, whatever God has called you to do, wherever he places you, do it all to the glory of God. Let your light shine. Bring hope. Bring Jesus. Anywhere. Everywhere.

REFERENCES

Bowlby, J. *A Secure Base*, 1988.

Bowlby, J. *Attachment and Loss*, 1997

Brown, J & Christensen D. *FAMILY THERAPY Theory and Practice,* 1986.

J. Brown & L. Errington (Eds) *Bowen Family Systems Theory in Christian Ministry*, 2019.

J. Cohen, A Mannarino, & E. Deblinger *(Eds.) Treating Trauma and Traumatic Grief in Children and Adolescents, 2nd Edition,* 2017.

Gordon, T. *Parent Effectiveness Training: The Proven Program for Raising Responsible Children.* 2019 Edition.

McGoldrick M. & Gerson R. *Genograms: Assessment and Intervention,* 1985.

Minuchin, S. *Families and Family Therapy, 1974*

Rogers, C. *On Becoming a Person*, 60th Anniversary Edition, 2004

Rogers C. & Farson, R *Active Listening, 1957*

The Bible. English Standard Version, 2016 Edition

Webster-Stratton, C. *The Incredible Years, 2005*